Viola Wendt was born in Boise, Idaho, in the last city block before the foothills began.

Her earliest memories are of flora and fauna: Sagebrush, sheep ticks, coyotes, sweet peas and pansies in Idaho and cats, mice, rabbits, frogs, birds and spiders in Wisconsin, where her family came when she was seven years old.

After schooling in West Bend, Wisconsin, she earned her bachelor's degree at the University of Wisconsin-Madison. There, in her junior year, she was told she had a "talent for the bizarre," a quality evident in the comic-satiric strain in her later writing.

During a year of graduate work at Radcliffe College, the Depression broke, interrupting her plans. "There were jobs and non-jobs during the Depression," she says; at one time her "immediately available resources" were 78 cents. While getting her teaching certificate, she was "a live-in factotum and child-sitter."

She earned her master's degree in 1936 and her doctorate in 1947 from the University of Wisconsin-Madison. Miss Wendt taught at Madison and Platteville State Teachers College until 1942, when she came to Carroll College in Waukesha, Wisconsin. She retired from Carroll in 1975 as a professor of English.

Miss Wendt's poetry-writing began, she says, when she was nine years old. ("I woke up one morning," she wrote, "with a poem in my mouth.") Since that day she has had several poems published; "On Reading Marianne Moore," published in the *Beloit Poetry Journal,* won a national honor, the 1955 Borestone Mountain Poetry Award.

"But somehow," she says, she "never took part in the politics of publication until a swan song was appropriate. Ironically, retirement is triggering new poems."

You Keep Waiting for Geese is her first book.

Miss Wendt teaches a writing course for women over 25 years old. Her hobby is portrait photography.

YOU KEEP WAITING for GEESE

YOU KEEP
WAITING
for
GEESE

Selected Poems
of
Viola Wendt

Wood Cuts
by Mona Noe

Carroll College Press
Waukesha, Wisconsin

Library of Congress Catalog Card number: 75-29746
ISBN: 0-916120-01-5 (cloth)
      0-916120-02-3 (paper)

Printed in the United States of America

Acknowledgements: To *The Beloit Poetry Journal*
for permission to reprint "Late Afternoon Landscape in
January" and "On Reading Marianne Moore"; and
to the National Council of Teachers of English for
permission to reprint "To a Teacher of Poetry-Writing"
from *College English*.

The writer cordially thanks Chad Walsh, Gordon R.
Folsom, Manfred G. Wuerslin, Herman Salinger and
Robert W. Wells for critical reading of the manuscript.

To the persons and creatures
living and dead
who have shared my life

Contents

This symbol, ✷ , is used at the bottom of a page to indicate a space between stanzas.

You Keep Waiting
for Geese

On the Coming of Age

Phoenix Night

Fortieth Birthday

This is the phoenix night, the night of fire.
The old bird of youth, womb-oriented,
mounts the pyre. His iridescence flames;
the ashes fall. Within their warmth the new
bird of age flaps his dusty wings.
His eye is homeward, his focus is the grave
now on this phoenix night, this night of fire.

Aubade

With the alarm of returning light,
and the cry of the robot beside the bed
repeating our brave evening intent,
our grave and deliberate act of faith—
we turn from the tension of night, from dreams
in which the increasing dead come back
with no surprise, and touch and speak;
where the gratification of love is free,
where logic and time bend to desire
and chaos dissolves the shape of law.

As we wake we remember at once
what world this is, light, real.
We are not confused; we know the dead
are dead, that love may be lost or wry,
that acting and suffering wait for us
whether decreed by physics or God.
We have learned that the daily tabula rasa
of the child is not for us; the past
is on our backs and in our bowels.

The memory of our Gethsemanes
has wrought a peace. We look on our graves
quietly now. We have forged a cross
on which something hangs. We are therefore content
enough to see the light come in
and to quit our beds for another dawn.

Decade

Aged fifty-one:
in the west, is the sun
colder, and thin in the eye?

Aged fifty-two:
something is due—
but where is the debt set down?

Aged fifty-three:
whatever you see
in the peep-show will cost you a penny.

Aged fifty-four:
you'll go no more
where the violets all are plucked.

Aged fifty-five:
you won't get out alive,
but the dying has its own dark relish.

Aged fifty-six:
the cosmic fix
augments the private dilemma.

Aged fifty-seven:
you'll never get to heaven
in the time that's left.

Aged fifty-eight:
the penultimate
odor of lavender thickens.

*

Aged fifty-nine:
you must take a little wine
for your stomach's sake.

    Sixty years old:
    yet the mended bowl
    still comes cold from the well.

Declassified

Who can tell Lear from the Fool
or either from the Wise Old Man
of the archetypes?

I have shucked my stereotypic skin
and hung it up on the south line-fence
where it soughs in the wind.
I am now, in old age, not obliged
to particularize my being—
or even, indeed, to *be*
(in my decade, dying's a decent event).
Moreover, chief among incident boons:
as sage or as clown, I may say whatever I will.

The young have their need of identity crises.
Olding, I relish my nonentity,
gratefully declassified
in this nameless lull
between file and shredding machine.

—For Jacob Van Tuinen, who remarked that one of the compensations of aging is
being able to say whatever you want.

Watering Plants in Old Age

Once I watered my potted plants
on every Saturday afternoon
in a week of decent duration.

Now it seems always Saturday afternoon.

Vague intervals only of other acts
lodge on my memory—
reality now
is the watering of plants.

Time in old age is a dropless stream,
riftless and solid.
Faster it flows and faster, till soon
I shall be standing forever
on an endless Saturday afternoon
my green thumb on a watering can
pouring an uninterrupted jet
of days and nights
onto my purple and crimson plants
as they overburgeon their pots
and, bloated and rank,
rot at last from solicitude.

Good Company

Having failed to create God
by returning His favor
and making Him out of clay
and my own living breath,
I tried a presumably lesser project:
finding myself some friendly angels—
for I urgently needed something
in the line of Presences
in my empty house
to warm and comfort my terminating.

"Turn but a stone, and start a wing!"
is said of the ubiquity of angels.
I turned over stones a summer long,
but all I started was slugs
and miscellaneous darters and creepers—
never a wing.

Angels, it was clear, are not found;
they too must be made.

Shifting tactics,
I forged in my brain a classic image
of radiant, white-robed epicenes,
wingèd, splendid, impassioned,
compassionate, learned, witty, wise—
good psychic company
on the road to death.

From this creative strain
pressure built up in my brain-pan.

*

One winter night
out of a small Zeus-crack
in the skull
came four little winged things—
epicene, likely;
but sparrowy, grey, unpretentious, frail.

I raged and wept.

Yet my ambience now
is filled with comfortable flutter,
with warm and engaging company.
On each bed-post
a Presence perches:
the nights rejoice
and death may come when it will.

Old Cat

Death is God's artifact, not mine:
He had it rigged and waiting
till the apple should be bit.
Therefore let *Him* bleed Angst, sweat guilt,
cry culpa. *I* propose
to enjoy myself while I can
like an old cat
that purrs till the fire's out.

Death is none of me—
except to die:
why should I die each night
when once will be often enough?
At the crucial time God and my kin
can handle the needed disposal
according to modern technics
and ancient ritual.

Directives

The place of my grave is known.
It's recorded in documents
official and semi-legal.
The directives you find in my purse
will bring me unerringly there:
to grave #1, next to mother and father—
sister nearby. (#4 is untaken:
do you know of a need?)
You'll spot the granite monument
engraved with grapes—
Dionysos and Christ
amiably sharing a symbol.
Wherever I die: Jerusalem; Pferdsfeld;
Arlington County, Virginia;
or a nameless spot
where three roads meet—
they'll ship me back as requested
to rest in peace
among kith and kin
in the Washington County Memorial Park
on the outskirts of West Bend, Wis
in the U.S.A.
Zip Code 5
3095

Low Hedges

Matthew Arnold at 65
leaped over a low hedge
and came down dead
on the other side.

How good a way to go:
how quick and clean.
A gift of God, it is said,
for both the dead
and his friends and kin.

But you note how carefully,
since Matthew Arnold,
the old walk around
low hedges.

Portable

Thank God
it's my *left* elbow that's arthritic:
that shrieks at the merest graze,
vibrates like a tuning fork,
unbuckles my fingers
from handles and pins,
and grates, like an abandoned windmill,
against rust and accreting lime,
the poor man's marble,
his portable gravestone.

Invitation to the Party

The flies have been venting their excrement
    onto the birthday icing,
bespeckling its rosebuds, crusted and dyed—
    and the cake's now ripe for slicing.

Come gather round the feast, my friends,
    (such as aren't in earth reclining);
there'll be candle and cake and fly-specks and flies,
    and the Devil to share your dining.

Variations on a Theme

Come, Sweet Death

"Now more than ever seems it rich to die,
    To cease upon the midnight with no pain."
      –Keats: "Ode to a Nightingale"

Let's Go!
    We've got our scripts;
    we're letter-perfect
    and cue-perfect,
    rehearsed ad nauseam.
    For God'sake,
    what are we waiting for?
Let's Get The Show On The Road!

Lines on Socrates

Before he drank the hemlock
Socrates took a bath in the late afternoon
to save the women the trouble
of washing his body
afterwards.

He had the advantage of knowing
his deadline:
after sunset the warden,
amiable, distressed,
would bring the cup.
Socrates knew he could keep himself clean
that long.

I am devoting this summer
to cleaning my house,
ordering, labeling, throwing away,
so that those by law pre-designate
can ready it for others
to live in at ease
without mementos
of the spider who sat in the web,
the mouse who made a nest
of the scraps, the snips
of a lifetime.

But unlike Socrates
I have no deadline.
It may well be that just when the house is clean
the Boot will step on the spider,
the Trap will spring on the mouse's nape—
and the legal disposers praise their luck.

*

But it may be too that the evening sun
will linger like Joshua's noon
and the spider's web grow thick and dusty again,
the nest of the mouse assemble again
from the scraps of this late, protracted life
senile, disorderly.

In either instance—disengaged
from order, or clutter—
I shall check with Socrates himself
on just what it was that he found
when he left that clean body behind.

Holy Gas

Twice for me in a relatively longish
life the sacred effluvium
has spurted out from the Delphic gas-jet.

The first time as a do-it-yourself
priestess I spoke into the Cave
the then modish truth
that "God is dead."
                     I grew giddy.
Then, after psychedelic ecstasy
and coma, standard
procedure for Apollonian oracles,
I heard in the hiss of the gas these words:
Nonsense! He isn't dead.
He's mad.
          Nuts.
             Crazy.
                Off
His holy rocker.
               Be of good
cheer.

The second time, I polished up
an old query and spoke it for sport
into the sacred orifice:
What, O god of light and art,
is the key to a happy human life?

My quarter had hardly clinked to the base
of the vender than the godly answer,
impelled by a pious CO_2,
fizzed into my trembling paper cup:

*

19

Zeitvertreibung and *divertissement*—
to avert the eye from the Void:
busy work
and a short, a blessedly short
attention-span.

Pelias Updated

*On Whether to Seek Jungian Counsel
in Old Age*

Thessalian Pelias
did not leap from the bubbling pot,
for Medea had quickly decamped,
and the incantation that had friskied the old ram
had not been spoken over the herbless brew.
Pelias was dead,
goulashed in vain by his duped, love-desperate daughters.

Time-wizened now like Pelias
and numb with anomy,
should his avatar
hack-up himself for the same boiling gamble?

Would his Jungian sorceress say
the triggering words over the caldron,
and some succulent thing spring out,
a neonate self, charged with ardor
and pungent with herbs from the cunning earth?

Or, though without Medea's malice,
would the wizardess flub the witching—
and he be a kettle of cubed meat
that would soon grow foul, breed skippers, and rot?

"Easy Is the Descent to Hell"

The crest of the hill is an elixir. Taste.
It is good. Somewhere along the visible road
a grave is dug. It is mine. With exhilaration
I descend before an archetypal tail-wind.
The scenes of declivity glow through my spectacles
of symbol and system. I have tapped the racial source,
have reaffixed the ancient umbilicus.
Gusto and equanimity wash my members
and no surprise lurks in the amber decades.

I'll wrench you now any event
to my bed of lop-and-stretch.

. . . Beware the dream from the ivory gate!

Injunction

Old women who think they have wasted their lives
probably have.

But that's their concern.

Let them hide their conviction
under the crumbling bags
and brittle newspapers
stacked in their psyche's shack—
when they are dead
the city will take care of the rubbish.

Let them never carry
their frayed treasure
into public alleys
like palmed postcards
to solicit a prurient pity;
or flog themselves in the town square
hoping to induce
a delicious horror at the red
knout.

For who cares?
Hasn't everybody got his own problems?

Bile

The sewers of the city are bilious
with the yellow spew and rage
of its Senior Citizens.
Old woman there at the rim
of that manhole, move aside;
I too have an elderly
bellyful to vomit
into the common drains.

The stench, to be sure, is not good
for the city's children or lovers
or for the workers or governors.
How to quiet the queasiness
of the old: to appease the rage,
the despair? With high-rise, low-rent
housing: carpeted; fauceted
hot and cold? Free buses,
free movies, free snacks, abundant
cards and cronies? Free medical
kept-men to take in the slack
in the stretched elastic?
                         These
are civilized palliatives
and humane. But the guilt for age
and for death is not ours; it is God's:
He allows our senile bile.

Let the angry old, then,
puke in the lap of God . . .

    Or is the truth perhaps
    that, trapped like us in the Nature
    of Things, He is bilious too?

Dissembling

Elderly spinsters who are, so to speak,
unimpeachably unmarried
are packaged in seamless, adhesive cellophane
intactile, invisible.
You may see them, off guard
in sly moments,
clawing at it
as at bloody, rooted scabs.

Delusively cool and sleek,
it sears and corrodes—
the fiery gift,
inadvertent, unwitting
(but relished),
of the System's married Medeas
protecting their equities.

In public moments
the clouded maidenly eyes
dissemble acquiescence and cheer.

Seven Friends of a Certain Age

Seven hens in one hen-house:
tough-fleshed,
long past egg-laying.

Ligaments at the throat
like binder-twine—
or heat-holding
yellow
belly-fat
under the grey feathers.

Scrawny or plump,
they'll all be a long time in the pot
when their turn comes to boil.

If it weren't that God seems to enjoy
His whole creation
just for itself
one might sometimes at twilight
beside the contemplative lamp
wonder what these seven hens
provide
in creation's economy
other than soup.

One chick, to be sure
(though 1:7's a shabby statistic),
did come out of the lot of them.

Besides, seven's a magic number—
even a sacred one.
And surely God's benevolent pleasure
is warrant enough for these seven hens.

A Little Time

I have a little time left.
Whom can I friend
in those minutes or years
in the sun,
in the rain?

I smelled lilacs once
with a man who is dead.
Do you know, old woman,
how many smells there are
in a lilac grove?
For every color a different smell:
lavender, azure, purple, mauve,
violet, white, and almost red,
pink, and almost pink . . .
single, double, and whorled.

We smelled them all
on that golden day,
green day:

two fragile butterflies
drifting on redolent drafts
from bush to bush,
Persian to French,
purple to white;
two lonely dogs
vainly sniffing the urine of God
to decode His holy
cryptograms.

The time that is left
is short.
          Has someone planted
          a lilac tree on his grave?

Spring Light

Now in the light of May there are greens
like the various touch of love, and an open
and endless blue in a gold enchantment.

In the young, desire spins like a slot
machine, and jack-pot love spills
in the snatched noons and the timeless dark.

For them the touch is substantive,
and the violent light reflects the moment's
joy and the somber compulsions of youth.

For us who are old this exquisite light
is tempered by death and renunciation
and pain, and the multiple face of God.

Yet our ecstasy is greater than theirs—
poignant and counterpointed by beauty
and terror in the anguish of golden light.

Unexpected

She hadn't expected that ever again would her aging
bones be liquid with love, that winter moonlight
would spill its silver stream into the old,
dry runlet long abandoned and boarded
over as unfit for bucket or cup. The sudden
water ran gratefully fresh and sweet.

Old man with silver hair radiant under the
snow-blooming trees like wild plum in the moonlight—
did your bones unexpectedly tremble too?

Word

All Creation is in me and wants its Word,
wants before death
its precise and passionate
lasting
and resonant Word:
fire and rock and the white arc of a gull.

But my only word now
is these little poeticisms
tatted of raveled lace
and moldy store string
left behind
by a grey, nidific sparrow.

I Have a Word

I have a word that is mine alone,
my *In Hoc Signo*, my *Om*,
to give life meaning
or make it tolerable:
Deedie.

Deedie in the voice of a child
and that child my daughter's son.
Blood of my blood, you know.
By a subtle dialysis
my aging blood is cleansed and renewed in his.
I am Deedie:
I know who I am and what.

I alone am Gramma Deedie
whom age cannot wither.
For the new little blood-kin tongue—
garbling my given name—
bespeaks my blest immortality:
Deedie.

—For Dorothy Sainsbury Steinmetz, who is Deedie

Let Me Hear What You Say

Left-over movers and shakers, my cronies;
relicts with a little honey, a little
song still in magnanimous mouths,
let us talk together and so make tolerable
this painful world. Peripheral now,
acquiescing, we move in our simpler orbits
and shake a slow leg in this unseemly
after-dance, for which the music
comes, fragile and dark, from afar.

Only words can make an order
out of this odd enigma of age
that came one sudden day with the sunrise.
Let me hear, then, what you say. Wisdom
on wisdom, perhaps we can build a benign
sub-world in which old women can live
with relish and grace, praising their twilight,
and a shrine's lares last until nightfall.

Embroidery Belongs to God Alone

To a friend who complained that her life, which should have become a lovely embroidered design, was only a chaos of colors and lines.

Embroidery belongs to God alone.
Your lot is tangled skeins and the rainbow
snarl of mill-ends, 1/3 off.

See how He lifts His needle of pure
silk, natural sheen, all of a dye-vat.
Your acetate fuzzes and mats
in lumpish asymmetry.

Yet you have seen His pattern,
have comprehended the fact
of embroidered order.
No more belongs to you.

Late Afternoon in Autumn

This is the hour of failure
when the light dies
and the leaves fall
and the heart quails
at the wasted year.

You Keep Waiting for Geese

When the leaves go
and the light fails in the fall,
you keep waiting for geese
high in their southering wedges
against the splintered sky.

When they come—
glittering and honking—
the listening air is pierced
by the beaks of the birds,
by their cold clairvoyant call.
In the strong wake of their wings,
high, high, and free,
follow the great white gods
of the wind and the snow.

The instinctual wedges cry
in a loud voice as they pass,
praising the South before them
and the white gods sweeping after;
praising year after year
their retraceable flight
in the wake of the sun.

But at last, slow in the autumn sky,
there will come a silent wedge,
their astute wings reading the invisible
One Way signs
as they head for a farther South
and a timeless Sun without motion or wake;
for a green garden where,
in a lazaret-aviary,
The Meaning sits
divulging Himself
in beauty and terror and tedium.

35

Love Is Loose in the Streets

On the Many Faces of Love

Love Is Loose in the Streets

Love is loose in the streets, my friends. Wear masks,
walk carefully. Love like an exhalation,
subtle as the pink light that lies
on the roofs on February afternoons,
droplets of light scattering the virulent culture
of endemic love, a serious infestation.
Beware, beware, my friends,
lest the beauty of your brothers seize you,
doom you to love in service and ecstasy.
There is no recovery. You will lie in your graves
pitted and scarred with the devastations of brotherly love.

Empathy

The breath-thin bones of the old,
their horn-tough toenails
and wanton bladders,
their frail and comic egos,
their periscopic, Lazarine eyes
that grope around the final Corner
and come back daily in fear—
and acquiescence—
these she understands.
By empathy
        she becomes old.

Without generation gap
she moves in the world of the young.
She knows how it is down there
and all the way up
to tall whiskers and ubiquitous hair,
to mutilated jeans and penciled eyes.
She knows about make-believe;
about masks, like scabs
that cover the healing of proud wounds.
She knows about fun-things;
and about heavy doors that open.
By empathy
        she becomes young.

*

She knows where it hurts
in ailing bodies and minds
and talks the language
of pain and fear and comfort.
Her hands understand what is soothing,
what feels good.
She knows what can be endured
with a little reassurance;
and what must simply
be endured without hope.
By empathy
        she becomes sick.

She understands the psyches and bodies of dogs:
the need for the exquisite scratch behind the ear,
the gentle thump on the rump,
the belly ruffle.
While the rest of us
protect our sanitations,
our acceptable smells
by friendly condescension and distance,
she moves in for a romp.
By empathy
        she becomes doggy.

—For Gwen Davies

Hour

The shadows of the moving feet
of water fall on mottled sand;
wind-thin and grey, the velvet spoor
creeps leeward on the yellow strand.

The under curves of rock are soft,
like green sea-kitten bellies furred;
the rippled little hair is sleek
with shadowy water, wind-bestirred.

For one of two who softly wade,
the sun in yellow light sets free
an hour of gold unloneliness
from out her dark mortality.

Absence

The light grows greyer, softer;
the rectangles of evening
move in my window
from luminous to dark
and the air is cold.
The bricks grow black
in the angled abstraction of night.
The metal hours strike in the shadow.
And you are not here.

Anomaly

Dear colleague in anomaly,
come, can we pray, are we honest?
What are the meanings of lives
like ours between two worlds?

Christ that had life is gone
like a centipede crushed in the carpet.
How then shall I pray, invoke
the universe to keep you?

There have been dead gods before,
and Love is older than Paul.
Therefore in simple faith
I have prayed that God should bless you.

Elegies for Ruth

Brightness Has Fallen

Brightness has fallen out of the universe
into a little dust. God is diminished
by this loss, and love goes defective
into eternity.

The spring that has come again
is darker now and cold.

To One Killed Driving an Automobile

Didn't you know, Icara dear,
it was only wax that held those wings;
that physics and not the fervor of sun-fain
spirit must govern Daedalean gear?

Passionate one, long in our fears,
the sun has burned as it must. Now wings
and will and exquisite spirit lie
under the weeping of our tears.

To a Psychiatrist Treating a Woman
of Mature Years

Father and Uncle and God,
lay your hand on the head
of this little female child
and teach her how to love.

Surrogate out of time,
alter the faults of years;
teach the child to be loved
and the woman to have been loved.

Forgive God's iron face
its father image, His Calvin
heart its mother mask
of unlove, which petrifies.

O wrench the years, and by love
ungrave the terrible stone.
Vicegerent of timelessness,
redeem this loveless time.

Ode to a Trope

Now it is spring again, my salamander,
    and this singular one-way love of mine
    flames into fire. O incombustible,
    cool, cool, my long inviolate myth.

O poignant trope of a greater Salamander—
    I have burned against the heart of Christ, the sacred
    adamantine Heart. Impervious, too,
    He is uninfringed among the cooling stars.

Unrequited

Desire turns in its follicle
like a too-much plucked hair.

The rocket shoots from its stand
then sputters and plummets.

The pinkening buds abort
and are sloughed from the bough.

Have you heard the mourning dove
sing with a cleft tongue
her four notes like a prison?

I have loved you too many unrequited winters.

Career Woman

Her married sisters and peers eat privately
at their nuclear tables. Their mouths are blessed; their teeth
are full of nuptial meat, their laps of crumbs.
They feel the honey in their throats; and when the chairs
are tilted back, satiety contents the eaters.

Her lot is to sit with men in their civic talk
while they pick their teeth in the forum; their public breaths
are redolent of that private meal in the kitchen.
Her teeth, unabraded, are sharp; she has learned perforce
to spit between them in a long and decorous arc.

Landscape Seen from a Room

What does it all mean: the long light
shot back from the glittering cock on the church,
the glisten of sun-glazed windows, the exquisite beige
of birch trees gilt by the sun, red caboose,
blue-grey horizon, white sift of snow—
what does it mean, what can it possibly mean?

I turn to my sawdust love who stands at my shoulder.
Propping him up more firmly by stick and by string
I take my strength from him. We ask: Is this beauty
substantive? . . . Are there theophanies here? . . .
Are these sun-shot panes the cataracted eyes of Hell?
The straw at his tied wrist tickles my ear.

I am made secure. We have asked these questions together,
he and I. I am not alone. The terror
under the leaf, the void beyond the horizon,
the ashless nothing left of matter and value—
these are forgot. For the universe is filled
with his presence. I can face the dark with poise and with love.

O stuffed one, stay. Lean always over me.
If you go, there is only God for company,
only God at my back, leaning, filling
the world with a cold and empty loneliness
that I could never bear. O beloved construct,
my straw-built love, do not leave me alone.

Defense

Engaging flowers, the white violets
turn up their softly fragrant throats.
An aging spinster can endure their smell
with only a little pain:
a delicate smell, close-clinging,
chaste—or almost chaste.

The apple blossoms are harder to take:
their pink fragrance diffuse
on the soft wind,
less chaste, and heavy with old regret.

Most anguishing are the lilacs,
their pervasive smell the smell of desire
at its most primitive.
The spinster defends herself as she can
against their wanton purple.

Deus Interruptus

Exult on the drum!
Be glad on the flute!
The Lord High God is abroad—

My bush is about to burn!

After a winter of accidie,
as torpid as Adam before the holy Breath
first got into his lungs,
my bush has erupted a red spurt
out of a nether node.
Soon God unconsuming will blaze
from this bloody floret;
this blossom will seethe into flame
while my bush crackles and shudders
unconsumed.

There! A thrust of light!
A spit! A sizzle! . . .

Then silence . . .
My bush with its
promissory bud
is cold again.

Abashed, I bend to examine
the rosy jut from the nodule.

There I find
a little red
straw
flower, stuck
on the stick
with a pin.

Late Afternoon Landscape in January

Now the slant of light in the afternoon
refutes the atheist. For the eye of God
is at tender angle under the breasts of snow
and His holy hands are soft on the white rumps;
purely now the libidinous innocence
of holy, rosy fingers finds delight;
and, passim, over the acquiescent land,
for His lovely lust in the violet afternoon
the montes veneris rise, with tracery
of shadowy twigs on the flushed, inviolate snow.

Narcissus

When the crystalline surface
began to flaw
the water was roily at first
and the image was intermittent.
Then the silt rose
and the murk
allowed but a thick
outline.
Then the pasty mud
obscured all image.
Now Narcissus
leans as always—
staring at baked slabs
caked up
from the dry bottom.

Obtuse

She had learned blanket-fluttering
to send him smoke signals,
and prosody to write him verses.
But smoke was not among his languages;
and he never knew
that the crafted lines she sent him
were love poems.
Indeed—
if Lady Godiva,
her long patrician hair coifed elegant and high,
had reined her warm white horse
before his very eyes,
he would not have known
that she was naked.

What It All Comes To

As mice in their
rubrics of security
cherish
the obsessive concept
of hole,

so these men
who scuttle into our straw
are risibly,
rodently
hole-obsessed.

Liberated Lady-Solipsist

. . . besides,
who needs
anybody else—
what with one's own ears
within earshot of
one's mouth,
and those delicious
titillations,
the much-touted *frissons*
built-in
and available
by taking just
a modicum of trouble?

Psychiatrist: First Poem

Acquainted with grief and known to pain,
seared and rendered compassionate
by the lonely hells that spend their hour apiece
in the day's assembly line before her desk,
wise in the hybrid wisdom of man and God,
she gives to God and man and chemistry
their just and merciful due.

The Mary-pity of her voice
drops on the head bowed in the chair,
on the hands before the eyes—
taking the dry self unaware with a flooding and kindly anguish
that comforts and liberates. By love she understands
the terror and the labyrinth; and so persuades
to singleness and peace.

She walks in love beside her patient-child
into that ultimate place—
there where the inscrutable stone gives back
silence, only silence, nothing, the wind across the sod,
the empty glare on the grass, on the snow;
or the barely endurable sound of a man's eternal soul—
there where beyond his will a man must listen
and hear what he can hear.

Psychiatrist: Second Poem

Looking at the world and seeing that it was a bad
bet, first she anchored her craft to the leeward
of God, and then she laughed. The foolish ways
of flesh, the somber compulsions of blood, the fog
and vagary of mind drew her pitiful Marian tears—
and then her laughter, the primitive sun-frank laughter
of earth; and the ribaldry of one who knows
the sly dark undersides of many lives.
She gave the world her wit, literate, wise,
shaped by court and church and tavern and cell,
the sword-play of ten thousand years of words;
pert firecrackers; and the grim and humorous
comment of man on the life he is given to live.

Kinsmen

On the Creatures
with Whom We Share the Earth

August Sequence Under the Lamp

Trespass

Night after night
diminutive kinsmen,
dropping on frail translucent wings
to the lighted white page
stained with my heart's ink,
strutted awhile on my desk,
flexing their minuscule muscles,
and died.

Indulging the winsome trespass
I saw in dismay
the stumble,
the curling of little legs,
the gallant struggle,
the upright moment of triumph,
the collapse,
the stillness.

After a moment for their lying in state,
I gave them each a word of farewell
from a universe they never knew they were in,
a kinsman's committal to a grave in my ivy pot—
that my grieving pencil dug
deeper than their little need.

Coup de Grâce

This kinsman I know at once:
leggy, thrusting before her
a stiff and pointed reamer.

*

With crushed and wary paper
I shadow those six thin legs
attached as by suction cups to my page.
She fights to get off the runway,
one leg free, five bouncing on springs,
her little motors
seemingly all conked out.

Then in a spurt she is gone,
my ambushing hand slow, foiled.
Frustrate, I rue that sucking
dagger she has lifted free.

After a time she is suddenly there again
lying on her back, her six little legs,
crooked at the knees, waving upward.
Vainly she revs her motors.
Her frame quivers awhile in frail spasms;
then it is still.
I say her a requiem not unmixed with rejoicing
for that decommissioned proboscis
among the unmoving hairs.

Too soon! In one leap
the creature is airborne.

She returns crumpled
and wracked with small tremors.
With mixed compassion
I give her the coup de grâce
of courtesy and fellow-feeling—
proboscis and all.

Ark

A bright-green fellow of half-inch substance
arrives: two fitted sets
of glistening see-through wings,
iridescent, faintly ribbed,
and neatly crimped at the edges;
backward-curving antennae
like frail wires, electric-trembling;
and black eyes bulging from a narrow head
that swivels at the tip of the basic worm.

Crazy, dizzy, or frenzied,
he careens on my paper,
a spangled acrobat,
a satyr in god-drunk ecstasy.

After an antic while
his little turn has come
to join our kinsmen under the lamp:
God's living breath
all gone out of their nostrils;
their pale antennae
limp on my written words.

A moth comes bumbling, flopping,
aeronautically disadvantaged
under the gooseneck.
I barely greet him,
my PR energy exhausted.

Then a cricket comes, quietly walking,
black, sedate.

*

Great God, is the whole Ark coming to call—
and to die under my lamp?
Aghast, I put out the light and run.

In the morning, under the cold lamp,
the moth body lies powdery dead.
And I am alert for cricket-nips
in my paper and cloth—
or a small corpse dry in a corner.

Kinless

I stay my turning finger
till he shall get off the page I am reading—
this delicate spring-green body borne
on legs frailer than hair.
I reread the page, waiting
for this kinsman in the
universe of breath
to go elsewhere, to be
about his quivering little business.

He delays,
evaluating with trembling antennae-threads
the print I am reading for a third time
(his diaphanous wisp of presence
does not impede my eye).
I ponder in vain how to hurry him,
for how shall one nudge
so fragile,
so mini a posterior?

*

At last his survey satisfies
his mote of brain.
He stands on tiptoe and rises,
a small, pale-green helicopter,
into the hazardous air.
Here desire whelms him:
in his heart's unreason
he hurls his little succulence
onto my study-lamp.

No spot of him remains;
and I am alone and kinless.

Mourning Dove

This monoglot sits in my tree
grieving her wretchedness
through every daylight hour,
turning her crank of woe.

God's silly bird broods
on His holy, global egg;
quivering our ears with the news
of Abel's grave, and of ours.

My comic Paraclete,
be quiet, O stop, be still!
Hatch out God's addled egg if you will—
but hold your tongue, and give the daylight peace.

Four-Letter Birds

These pigeons outside my window—cooing, simpering,
histoplasmotic, and shimmering pigeons—
call out the National Guard, I say,
bring in the licensed police with shotguns
and shoot them, shoot them all. Let blood and feathers
fall in a red and grey-white mottled rain
down to the hard cement-way underneath.
There let them die, all of them die.
Then at last I'll have peace, be free
of their cooing and copulating,
their defecating down from the drainpipes;
their idiot cooing, their mongoloid cooing.
How can such glittering birds, burnished birds,
cunningly feathered, feathered surely by God
in His guise of Artist, make such sounds,
absurd and mournfully simple-minded sounds?
And those avian guts, miracle manufactories
of excrement, how can they make such messes
of mottled feces, turning these private and decent
window sills into a lewdly public
defecatory?

Bring on your rivers, O Hercules!

On a Picture with a Dove

Through the glass
one sees the urban angles
of high-rise windows
disappearing upward under the Venetian blind
and, at eye level,
of roof-tops and ventilators
from an earlier stratum of city.

The picture is done in varied greys and tans,
beiges, browns, a hint of blue.
In the lower right on the window sill
sits a bird in mixed grey
with a focal body-nimbus
of soft off-white.

His shrewd black eye
and confident beak against the pane
establish a persuasive nexus
with the eye behind the glass.
This bird of the city streets,
this Dove in an emblematic aura,
knows, subliminally,
that he is 1/3 of a God;
and he waits for the window to open.

"Cock in a Shower"

His stained-glass feathers washed
and sleeked in the rain,
his blood-gorged comb and wattles firm,
he thrusts his beak pertly into the sky:
he knows what he is and who.

He is that comely creature
who postulates a Creator.

Congenial to his cockiness,
this metaphysical role
exhilarates him;
he performs it with gusto.
(Shall God permit ambivalence
in His flamboyant positer?)

—18th century Japanese print: British Museum.

71

Trope

On the eye of a young she-camel
in a drawing in the writer's study

Grey-eyed
cow-eyed
—you remember your Greek goddesses—
this young she-camel
in her dark, preliterate eye,
a liquid and tender arc,
knows something that you don't know,
or at least Something is known here—
or knows Itself.

A Humorist
with a bent for the different drum,
the Great Metaphorist
intimates
by singular vehicles
His saving Mystery—
for salvation comes, at best, by trope.
His very Being is cued here
in the soft grey eye
of a pre-pubescent she-camel.

Cranes Descending

The cranes and the snow fall together
out of the evening sky:
five white birds diminishing
from near and large on the brighter horizon
into the farther, darker air.
Down they come and down,
their calculating wings tilted and spread,
their landing gear extended and ready.

The snow falls—forever unmoving—down and down . . .
You will listen in vain
for the thud of their white, muted landing
as the great birds forever descend . . . descend . . .

—Japanese wood block print, "White Birds Flying in Snow," by Sho-son:
Bibliothèque Nationale.

Frog Autumn

Complementary to a poem with the same title by Sylvia Plath

Summer ripens, hot-hearted Mother.
She fattened us with her green
and gold. Our taut skins
glisten in the lessening sunlight.

For a few more basking days,
content, awaiting the dreamless mud,
we will blink at the cooling sun.
Our paean-croaks diminish nightly.

Nirvana nears. Our folk
desire the Mystery.
Sleep-fed on fat-stored flies,
we relish this chill, pre-vernal dark.

Summer Night

In the black grass
dartles of gold are lighting
fireflies the way to their cryptic matings.
Piercing the shadow of bushes, the sparks
flicker upward into the trees
until, at the torn twilit rims,
the glitter of delicate signatures
in erotic calligraphy
vies with the minor stars.

Urgently out of the distant marsh
throat-swollen frogs—
enraptured signalmen—
in a medley of speeds
pulse their dark telegraphy
into the amorous night.

In innuendoes
of charnel house
and sweet-orange grove,
courtly magnolia blossoms,
unfolded, ripe,
suffuse the dark
with elegant excitations to love.

Praise Him! Praise Him! Praise Him!

Crickets, cicadas, frogs, and toads—
and other ontologically wise old parties—
in summer and fall, but peaking in August,
all day long and into the night
make their loud multifarious statements
about the nature of Being.

Being, they avouch, is the audible praising of God:
they go at their holy assignment
with vigorous leg and tongue,
with wing and inflatable skin.

But so great is God
that a proper praise
would make an intolerable sound—
no created ear
could endure such adoring decibels.

Sacrificing the resonant praise
that His own tough ears would relish,
in mercy God mutes the paeans,
tempers the laud, for mortal ear drums.
All the sounds that you hear
have been softly and fondly deadened;
yet for the noisy ones
they are noise enough
        to proclaim His glory by day,
        His glory by night.

*

But think now
how it will be at that final time
when created ears have been toughened like His
and God can give up His kindly muting—
and the white night
is wild with vibration.

Then there will rise
the uninhibited racket of Being,
an undamped bedlam of sound,
giving our worshipful God His due,
His sacred, eternal, and infinite due.

There'll be beat and rasp and abandoned clatter,
plink and chink and unmuted chirr,
well-deep garrumph
and grandfather dialogue
obscene, deliberative, delicate, wise:
a gurgling, a gargling,
a gut-brown sound
parting the atoms of air.

Blacksmith-tinsmith-coppersmith blows,
a brassy clang, a rumple and crackle of foil.

The bong of Hell, and the ping
of stars no longer there.
A cry of throats
bearing the meaning of all the millennia
etched on the ancient face
of the swamp and the rock:
splendid
august
absurd
and terrible.

A laugh of awe and delight
hanging forever on all of the twelve hard winds.

Think now—and quail and rejoice.
For this holy ruckus shall last
through aeons of August nights
and into eternity—

    so great is He;
    so worthy of praise.

Passerby

On Art, and on the Human Condition

Passerby

Epitaphs in the manner of The Greek Anthology

1.

Passerby,
lay thy hand on thy pulse and be glad
remembering the joy
this nothingness once knew.

2.

Passerby,
seeing us all lie here equally quiet and rotten,
go back and ponder
upon Tweedledum and Tweedledee.

The Answer Is Not in the Back of the Book

The answer is not in the back of the book,
blunt to the thumb; nor, slyly lodged,
in the brain of the teacher; nor in folded notes
pressed by love into the palm;

nor in the geology of nicks
carved in the chairs. The boards have all
been erased and the maps are crazed. In the raveled
books no veronica sweats.

This being so, you must do your sums
quickly; and zip yourself up nicely
when you've been to the bathroom; and say
please and thank you; and blow your nose.

Come, smile now. See, I'm smiling.
—I shall have to punish you if you don't—
You're a big boy now and can walk across
the street all . . . by . . . yourself.

In Memoriam: Prexy

The scapegoat's gone now, boys. God's got him.
The hatrack of all our discontents has tumbled.
There's no one to blame now. The spittoon of spite
has been moved from its brassy corner by the Great Charman.

What will we do now, boys? How
can we properly hate ourselves with the ducking clown
gone from the canvas hole? How with no dog
to kick can we decorously exculpate ourselves?

It's anarchy now, boys. Every man must content
himself pro tem with his own guts to gnaw.

Portrait

In public relationships
he sees invisible dimensions
with a geometer's eye,
and principles hitherto non-existent
bloom in sun-gold chalk on a green blackboard.
In a quick percipient fiat
he engenders intricate runnels from man to man
for fluent speech to pass, and prudent intellect.

But in the interpersonal—
in the intimate touch of curious antennae
as of snails, or the whiskers and damp appraising breath
of donkeys meeting where amity determines
the safety of carts on a narrow defile—
he plays a metaphysical chess,
moving blind kings and deaf queens
for bloodless mathematics' sake.

Prudent

I peck and am pecked
on the pecking scale.
More pecked, however,
than pecking, I
have braced my comb
and alerted my eye—
though not forgetting
(a prudent hedge)
to file my beak
to a handy edge.

Epicene

Surely
a bona fide God could,
by fantasizing a succulent lemon, say,
have stimulated enough saliva
to do the job a second time.

He had done it once:
made a creature of earth and spittle
and activated him by a nose-to-nose
transfer of living spirit.

He could do it again.
Why impute to him all that
pseudo-Caesarean surgery,
that rib-removal?
The incising, it's implied,
was needed to get a rightly
symbolic raw material
for fabricating the inferior
flesh-of-flesh, bone-of-bone.

It was Yahweh—that anthropomorphic scarecrow
nailed together by worthy Hebrew patriarchs
to entrench their primacy
by a God-sanctified put-down—
who, for his own phallic and feudal reasons,
went along with their game.

*

But surely
it was a true God—properly
epicene, shrewd, no chauvinist tool,
understanding his own dignity,
with his technique unimpaired
and finding a plethora of proven materiel—
who made the second of his lovely creatures
as an equal, autonomous instance
of his holy know-how.

Radical

All over the country
the warm breasts of women
are falling with soft plops
into buckets.
Knives bleed
and monitors blip;
the breath of surgeons
comes hard through the sweat
under the masks of God.

Little Fish Boy

The key to aesthetics
is pattern.

A long-legged man,
wearing pants striped
in black and white
like ticking that once
would have covered a featherbed,
sat with legs ajar:
the stripes at the crotch-seams
joined each other
in a pattern
of order and beauty.

I felt like Pound's
little fish boy.

—Ezra Pound. The boy said of both a beautiful woman and packed sardines in a box:
"How beautiful!"

89

Harpsichordist

A precise and tinkling and tidy little man,
a slight tight little man, skull-capped in black
and parted hair, played to us some tinkling,
precise, and tidy little tunes. The nice
and decent feet of gaiety tippy-toed
up the keyboards and down, twangling and nipping
the delicate wires under the gilded lid.
Then his dainty little passions swelled to a monstrous
tinkle, a Lilliputian furioso,
like a kitten with pansy face snarling and lashing,
a velvet beast in a toy-shop fantasy.

Poetry

Among sugar-tits
the best is poetry.
Breast surrogate, sweet
and salivary, it soothes our fret.

Among security blankets
it enwraps most snugly;
however unraveling,
it warms us, and hides.

Now and again we are driven
to fling away these rags
and to scream abroad
the frank pain of our being.

But soon we fumble back
our rags from their flung corners,
reswaddle our nakedness,
and drain again the breasts of the White Goddess.

On Reading Marianne Moore

We had never guessed what lay
behind the corroding iron gate
    or the rose hedge of Dresden blossoms
        and inedible haws
        with the fruited promise of pomegranates
        but having a wholly other
        texture and function in the mouth;
or beyond the eaten rock wall
    that gave no evidence of its embrace:
        the tiny garden spot with the white wicker and the poodle
        or mushrooms exuding the spotted smell that seduces
            leprechauns to alien heaths
        or a stark, magnificent drop to a sea that groans
            in a timeless suck and spew
            with a décor of porpoises
            and the arcs of discontinuous monsters;
or where there was no barrier at all
    but a place that rose soundlessly
    while we turned our backs inadvertently
    to contemplate a word hanging
    suspended from the color of intellect by a slim silk
    spun out of its crystal entrails.

*

But once there, we found the countryside familiar:
we had spent our forgotten childhoods there;
or a little Platonic door awoke in the seamless wall
and we recollected the ecstasy of knowledge.

In a joyous nostalgia we clapped our hands
as the invisible abstractions and interrelations
became square or pink
or barked like seals or small dogs
or made the noises or silences
of innumerable odd or ordinary fauna,
or opened mouths in which we counted
the exact number of teeth that we had always known
were there but that no Pliny
had ever told us about.

On Hearing the Aging Marianne Moore
Read Her Poetry

It was a wholly delightful game
and everyone got his money's worth:
an amiable, lively, witty, smartly
couturiered little lady, olding
and palely orchided, spoke to us
and read us pieces of poetry
neatly punctuated by auntly
parentheses and collusive grins.

The sponsors said she was Marianne Moore.
This was a pious metaphysical fraud.
But no one held it against them; there was no
intent to deceive on anyone's part.

This pale wraith of a poet was not,
we knew, the maker of toaded gardens.
She persuaded us that it didn't matter.
The faint little lavender bird in our hands
charmed us enough. The crested, crimson
bird in a fourth-dimensional bush,
the gilt-and-mosaic-feathered bird
that fame had labeled Marianne Moore—
the ontologists might bicker about.

We all enjoyed this honest evening.

They Flew to Him

Club Ladies Thank the Professor
Who Has Made Them a Speech

They flew to him as in a garden
out of the delicate vents of flowers.
The air breathed with their fluttering,
their velvet struggle and glide.
Honey hung on their lithe tongues,
swelled from their red throats.

They moved their soft-furred feet
across his lips. Their wings,
nape-tender, brushed and cajoled
his quiet lids. His ears
trembled and sang deliciously
to their tiny march and stroke.

His senses fattened and swooned at the downy
swirl and swoop. Waving
their silk antennae they tangled and panted
escape from his hair. Again,
again, the deliberate quiver and beat
moved across his mouth.

To a Teacher of Poetry-Writing

You say:
"This half-nelson, now, is designed
exclusively for angel wrestling."
Or: "Here is how you gouge your knee
into an angel's groin to bring him
to groaning terms."
Or: "Thus is he pinioned and plucked;
thus is he subtly shackled and singed."

This you can teach—
what you cannot teach
is where angels haunt
the dark path above the gorge;
nor how to desire the hot heart
and the eaten strength of the foe.

Presences

1.

I sat with Quakers
in their timeless silence,
sceptical, nearly amused.
Yet at last, in all despite,
a Something stood in the doorway
and took up space
and breathed
and loved.

2.

I was a guest of friends at Carmel-by-the-sea—
in whose house, her only happy home,
Marjorie (who smelled of heliotrope)
lived on in ectoplasm.

The story was told that, chatting after dinner
in the room where Marjorie liked to rise
in mist along the fire-place bricks,
Padraic Colum, unprimed—but a Kelt—
had turned to his hosts and said,
"They're here, aren't They?"

I smelled heliotrope all night long,
the hair on my nape aghast.

Galway Kinnell read to us
first Whitman and then himself.
Dimensions and Presences
oddly lodged
in egg-reft hens,
heart-bloodied bears,
and a gut-payed porcupine
rose about the room
adumbrating
some man-God privity.

We left that bloody bestiary
celebrating ourselves—
and braced in gut and heart.

Christmas Eve

The twigs are shadowed brown on the new snow.
The moon is crisp; and the small, bright secular
stars take their customary places.

In the church a croaking Gabriel tells the complaisant
Maid her glorious fruitfulness. (Did God
then like any Jove lie with his nymph,
an Oread from stony Bethlehem?)

In pillow tubing and fringed and corded robes
the Magi come with incense, gold, and myrrh.
The little breasts of the angels are bound in tinsel,
their girlish eyes adoring Virgin and doll.

The littlest ones pipe their chorus at the wrong
time. A shepherd tangles his crook in his skirts.
The quiet man of God prays for the dead,
for the quick, for the ambivalent bereaved. The unwifed
usher handles the arms of women softly.

Snow is falling again from the wordless sky.

At a Symphony Concert: Rumors of the Homeland

Here the knowing displaced persons of the town
(yet all—or none—are displaced)
gather to hear the rumors, the echoes
of a homeland they have been orphaned of.

As the dark cellos cry and the anguished violins,
the bright flutes,
the drums like the beat of blood,
the townsmen remember (they think) the green earth
and the sun like love on its lap;
the living leap of water
in the cool of the evening,
the dapple of moon by night.
They taste in recall a savory ambivalent
fruit holding in its flesh
some immense corroding guilt,
some redemptive ecstasy.
The old men carry the flavor in their throats;
the old women remember the succulence
in their tentative teeth.
Both remember the sinuous glossy dapple
of irremediable words,
a glint of sun on sword,
a road's dust soft on their covered thighs;
in their shrewd eyes a hard knowledge.

The young will remember these things later.

The music softens
and the wind blows fresh
out of the homeland.
The sea that washes its shore
becomes wine-dark and luminous.
They seem faintly to hear

the surge of that sea,
the gust of that wind.
The curses of sweat and of pain lift for a while:
they are at home again.

The knowing music falters.
In the hay of a cattle-manger
a new-born child
has been abandoned.
They beat their hearts: *mea culpa, culpa*.
Yet they partly guess
that he will come to them again
on his own godly recognizance.
They do not know if they are glad of this.

When the music has stopped;
when the flutes and the violins are dead,
the trumpets, the drums, the bassoons—
the listeners will ask again:
have we truly come from afar?
or did some inscrutable need within
devise this green land
and the urgent road
and the ambiguous child?
What is our guilt? Our terror?
What is the lambent penumbra of joy
around that dark core?
Have we truly heard
this wind, and this sea?

Their ears will be stone.
Yet below these hard thresholds
it may be they will truly have heard.